Unbreakable

Overcoming the chaos of abuse and
healing from the fallout of suicide

Monroe Porter

authorHOUSE

AuthorHouse™
1663 Liberty Drive
Bloomington, IN 47403
www.authorhouse.com
Phone: 833-262-8899

© 2022 Monroe Porter. All rights reserved.

No part of this book may be reproduced, stored in a retrieval system, or transmitted by any means without the written permission of the author.

Published by AuthorHouse 10/25/2022

ISBN: 978-1-6655-6832-6 (sc)
ISBN: 978-1-6655-6831-9 (hc)
ISBN: 978-1-6655-6833-3 (e)

Library of Congress Control Number: 2022915177

Print information available on the last page.

Any people depicted in stock imagery provided by Getty Images are models, and such images are being used for illustrative purposes only.
Certain stock imagery © Getty Images.

This book is printed on acid-free paper.

Because of the dynamic nature of the Internet, any web addresses or links contained in this book may have changed since publication and may no longer be valid. The views expressed in this work are solely those of the author and do not necessarily reflect the views of the publisher, and the publisher hereby disclaims any responsibility for them.

If you had asked me at the beginning of my journey what it looked like to deal with some real-life shit, I would have told you to fuck off and mind your own business.

I would have tried to keep myself hidden for fear of being judged and for the feelings of shame that would have come with it. But because of who I am and the voice that I have found, I am going to tell you what my journey has been like. It is chaos; it is like running to the bathroom with explosive diarrhea, barely making it there in time, shit running down your legs with no bathroom in sight and you are intensely sweating. No, I have not ever personally experienced this, but I am sure it would be a shitty deal.

It feels like walking outside in the middle of winter and not realizing you are on black ice, when your legs come out from underneath you and you land flat on your back. It is riding down a hill, as you tuck and roll, hitting every single rock on the way down. It is like being in the ocean and a wave comes and knocks you on your ass, and then another knocks you down again and you are now held under the water because the waves keep coming, and you cannot get your footing right, and the shock is so unbearable that you have no words but only fear because it is so fucking cold. It is like running around a pool area to go check on laundry, only to run smack into a clear glass door that you did not see (yes, I have done this). It is laughing at your life because it is so fucked up on every single level and the way I survived was to find humor within it.

I look back now on the obstacles that I have faced over the last four years, and it is no wonder why I have gray hair. Ah, who am I kidding? I have had gray hair since I was eighteen. I have gone through many different transitions, and if you are anything like me, I am sure you have also gone through many different transitions and really have no idea what is going on in the world. That is always something I can rely on, never knowing what is going on in the world. That is my constant. Always wondering what the next episode of my life will be and deciding I am going to ride it out.

Up until this point, I did not understand the purpose of my trials and pain. I never felt like my story would serve a greater purpose. I realized this book is a part of my purpose. This book is to share my story so that I can hopefully entertain and be a guide through your own story. I hope that I can share with you how I managed to turn the tables around. I will share with you the uncomfortable, chaotically messy journey of putting my life back together. I hope to expose what happens behind the scenes while healing from trauma. I hope that you understand that trauma and loss have no road map. It was all a disaster and I made it to the other side.

The hope is that together, along with your effort, we can make some sense of your own disaster and come out shining on the other side, ready to take over the world.

All I ask is that you are completely honest with yourself, and in return I will be completely transparent with you. I no longer have anything to hide from and that has brought so much beauty to my life and to those around me.

I am different now; I am standing firm in my truth, and I am going to try and help you stand firm in your truth too. I am uncertain what your truth is in this moment, and it may take some time to figure out what that is, but you have what it takes to get to that point.

I am here to help you fight whatever battle is in front of you. Together we will face the chaos and make it your bitch. Becoming unbreakable is possible, but it does require hard work and effort on your part to get down and under the ugly parts of your story.

The following pages will have some explicit language that is used and some of the humor that is thrown around in this book may or may not be funny to you. My intentions are not to be hurtful to anyone, but this is some real-life shit and I had to make the best of it.

As we dive in, I need to mention that all my experiences are very personal, and my trauma led to time not tracking right. To try to help you grasp what is going on throughout the book, I wanted to share with you a brief timeline. This timeline happened over the course of nearly four years.

- Falsely accused
- Went to jail for 18 hours
- Leaving my home
- Filing for divorce
- House fire

- Domestic & sexual assault (being stabbed, beaten, suffocated, cut in front of the children, strangled)
- Fleeing my home state
- Returning to my home state
- Sentencing hearing
- Suicide of my youngest brother
- Spiraling downward fast
- Intense therapy
- Hoffman Process
- Major inner work
- My shine returning

It is such a whirlwind, as I am writing this out. I must admit that I did some research before starting this. I wanted to be certain that I was ready to put this story on paper. Honestly, the domestic and sexual assault traumatized me initially, but my brother's suicide is what made me decide I needed help. I reference my brother's suicide in many areas of the book. I wanted to be certain that I would not be retraumatizing myself by going through this mind fuck again!

And it turns out, I am exactly at the place in my journey that I need to be. Writing this out on paper takes bravery and honesty. It takes what I have learned from my experience and making it my truth. Writing this means having the ability to explore how I felt and the lessons I have learned throughout the journey. I made the choice to turn my pain into purpose.

Before we jump in any further, I need to caution you to be aware. Some things I have written about in this book may be a trigger for you. My goal is never to have a negative impact on your healing, but triggers are real, and your reactions to those triggers are just as real. Please know that my intentions, for this book, are to have a safe place for you to reflect on your own journey to healing.

Please be kind to yourself. If you are triggered, take a breather. Please remind yourself that, in the moments of my trauma, you are safe. Focus on your surroundings and bring yourself back to the present. I am almost certain that my book will bring out some heavy emotions and that you may be uncertain what they are. Use those emotions as a guide to show you where you still need healing.

CONTENTS

Chapter 1　Humiliation 1

Chapter 2　Shame 7

Chapter 3　Why I Stayed 13

Chapter 4　Grief 17

Chapter 5　Vindictiveness toward Yourself 25

Chapter 6　How I View Myself: Why It Matters 29

Chapter 7　Distractions: Not Denial 37

Chapter 8　Downward Spiral 41

Chapter 9　The Process 45

Chapter 10　How Others Viewed Me 53

Chapter 11　It Is All about You 59

Chapter 12　Boundaries 67

Chapter 13　No Contact 71

Chapter 14　Forgiveness 75

Chapter 15　The Adventure to You 79

Chapter 16　What Your Body Remembers 87

Chapter 17　Triggers 93

Chapter 18　Things to Remember 95

Chapter 19　My Lessons 105

Acknowledgments 109

Never Truly Broken 115

CHAPTER 1
Humiliation

Put your hands up! Their guns are pointing right at me. My towel drops, and I am only wearing a half ripped-off bra. Blood is running down my face; blood is on my body; my head is drenched in Bacardi; my feet are frozen in the snow; and I am vomiting. What the fuck is going on? I am screaming, "Get my kids out; get my kids out!" I have no sense of time or what is happening.

All I know is that it is the middle of the night, and I am terrified. I am sick to my stomach, my heart is racing, my hands are sweating, and I am having a tough time breathing. I get into the back of a squad car and am handed a blanket to cover up. I am then brought to the ambulance. All I can do is vomit and scream for my kids. It feels like hours go by; time is going extremely slow. Finally, all four of the children are brought into the ambulance. The littlest one is only in a diaper, and I start to weep. Barely able to move my jaw or twist my neck, I see the fear in their eyes. I start bawling.

The children are terrified. The humiliation and guilt start to roll over me. The anger and rage are clearly present, and I sob uncontrollably. I am fucking pissed. I start to wonder if he feels bad about making the kids witness the assault. Did he enjoy it? One of the children begged him to stop! What kind of monster would do this to children? No person should ever do this to a family. "You are going to watch me cut off your mom's head and rip out her tongue. You are going to watch me murder your mom." What in the actual fuck?

I am brought to one hospital, where they take initial pictures of my wounds and assess the injuries. I had several stab wounds and multiple cuts. The children are waiting with the officers in a secured area waiting for a family member to come pick them up. I am then transported to another hospital that is equipped to perform rape kit tests. I arrive to the hospital, and they call for a domestic violence advocate. It was the advocate that I had worked with previously.

The hospital staff take an assortment of pictures of me naked. Pictures from all different angles. Pictures of the stab wounds, cuts, bruises, and scratches. Pictures of where my hair was cut with the knife and my least favorite, I was swabbed to gather DNA from the rape. I was anally raped. In between all the assessments, I had talked to the investigator, the sheriff, the domestic violence advocate, and many hospital staff. There were many people who were involved in this process. In those moments, I felt worthless. I felt severely humiliated. Talk about hitting every single rock on the way down the damn hill. Fuck those rocks. I did not like feeling bare, I did not want anyone to see me in the condition that I was in. I was embarrassed of what had happened to me.

Time seemed to go on forever when I was working through my sexual assault and my abuse. This process was complete torture. Being raped is not a one-time thing. It is not a one-time experience that happens, and you move on from it. Being sexually assaulted fucked with me mentally, physically, and emotionally. I was violated, not just my body but my mind and soul. My mind was killed; it was shattered. The stability that I once knew as a reality was killed. The life I knew was taken from the children and me. My coping mechanisms went down the drain.

What people do not understand is an assault, such as rape, completely changes you. There was a betrayal of trust. Everything about you is altered. It led me down a path of uncertainty, guilt, shame, humiliation, and doubt. I felt unclean and dirty. This was exceedingly difficult for me to come to terms with. This was something that I tried to hide from. I tried to block it out. I did not want people to view me differently or feel pity for me. I hated people feeling sorry for me. I did not view myself as a victim; I knew I would come out a victor. I knew in my heart that I would not let anyone else's actions towards me, or the children defeat me. I knew I was stronger than what happened to me. I had that fire in my soul to overcome what was done to me.

Something that was helpful to me while in therapy was working on my narrative. We broke down my narrative and did this in steps, to help me uncover my own underlying emotions connected to the rape. If you are unfamiliar with what a narrative is, it is a technique that is used to try to help you understand or make sense of what you had just been subjected too. It is used to uncover or expose your memories of the experience and make sense of it. With trauma there are so many memories or thoughts and sounds that are all intertwined together. What I learned is that I was dealing with many emotions of shame, something I will discuss in the next chapter. I was also dealing with anxiety, PTSD, suicide ideation, and had a negative self-image. I was mostly being vindictive toward myself, something I will discuss in Chapter Four.

I just want to remind you that, despite all that you may have gone through or are going through, there are many resources that are available to help you deal with the trauma. I used therapy as my go to for learning how to heal and make sense of things that made no sense to me. Within my therapy sessions I used a combination of CBT (Cognitive Behavioral Therapy) and neurofeedback.

No matter how much you may be struggling with something right now, it does not mean there is something wrong with you. It means you have pain that needs to be sorted out. It means there are things going on within you that need to be faced head on.

My hope is to raise awareness of the affects that trauma causes to people. My hope is to help you feel connected, seen and not alone.

Are you ready to speak your truth? For what are you fighting? Your life? Your kids? Your job? Your sanity? Your safety?

_____
_____
_____
_____

Take Aways:

- Humiliation is an asshole, and it will follow you around until you face it
- Sexual assault affects you in many ways and sometimes it is hard to verbalize what you are experiencing
- Uncovering your underlying emotions that are connected to your trauma is a safe way to healing
- Resources are available and beneficial
- Remember you are NOT at fault for someone else's behaviors

CHAPTER 2
Shame

I was so ashamed of what had happened. I was ashamed because I blamed myself. How could I let something like this happen to me? How could I let the children experience something so horrific? How did I not see things escalating? Why didn't I leave sooner?

What I did not understand in those moments, is that it had nothing to do with anything I did. I was ashamed because I let myself believe the lie, I told myself that it could never get this bad, when in fact many different situations of this same nature were this bad. I lied to myself for years. My pride was too big to allow myself to believe I had bad judgement. I turned my head to multiple red flags repeatedly. I was ashamed of myself for trying to make things better.

After years of dealing with trauma, I had no sense of who I was anymore. I was being told that I was crazy, that I need help, and everything was a game to me. I was so mentally distraught that I would take a shower and realize when I got out, I had only shaved one leg. Being distraught because I could not slow my thought process down enough to think clearly. I would go to work and realize that I had two different shoes on. I stopped trusting my own judgment. I heard all the rumors people would say and almost believe them. I felt defeated, with no sight of light at the end of the tunnel. This was all enough to drive my mind fucking crazy. It was enough to make my mind spin, and the crazy train seems never ending.

People can become so consumed with feeling the shame and punishing themselves for not making the right choice or not knowing the right answer. In a sense it provides you with control over something in your life when everything else is falling apart.

Shame is an immensely powerful and overwhelming state to be in. It can be crippling. I had plenty toward what I had endured. Here is one example of my shame. I am broken; therefore, I am unlovable. I went through this vicious cycle. After the assault, I felt broken and embarrassed to be out in public in my town. I went through this cycle of shame like this, only for the cycle to repeat itself repeatedly.

I typically started my shame cycle with an emotion I was having or a thought about myself that I was having. None the less, the shame cycle was difficult for me to manage, until I got to the core of where the emotion or thought was coming from. Shame sucks. Shame drains the life out of you. It is hard to understand and even harder to manage.

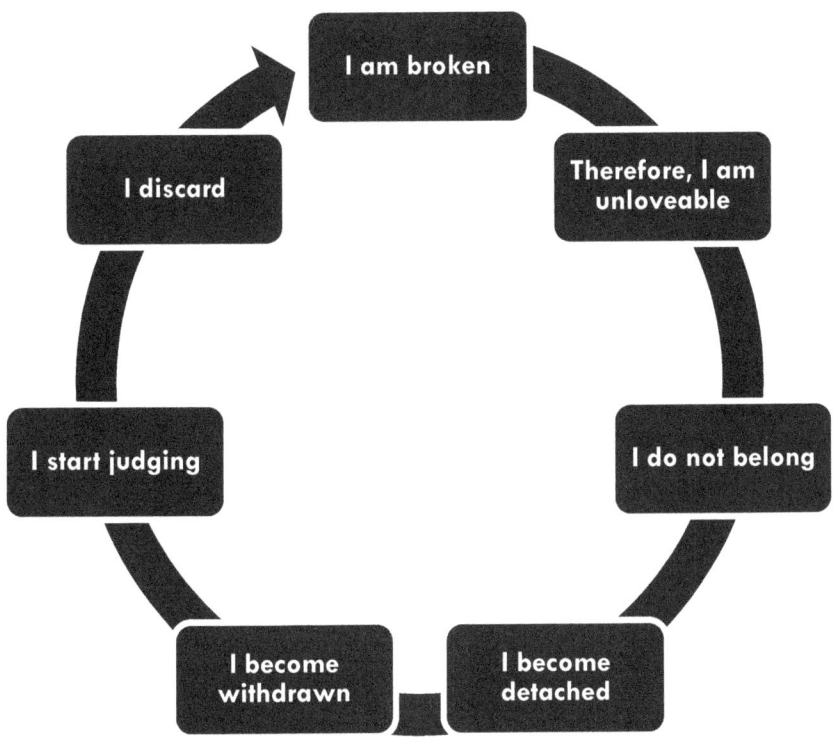

I carried a lot of guilt and shame with my brother's death because I held myself responsible. I was the closest one to him, and although I knew he was struggling, I told myself that I should have tried harder. But the truth is that I would not have been able to save him.

To be able to change this thought process and to have a successful transformation of your mindset, you must acknowledge that there is a problem. How does the problem affect you? Then you must forgive, not only yourself but those who have wronged you. Then comes exchanging your old mindset with something new—a new way of living. Obviously, the other ways of reacting are not working for your good.

I needed to claim the ownership of my life back and my right to self-love. Do you? You have the right to change your narrative. You have the right to want better for yourself and for the ones you love around you. You get to decide if you want to continue to go down the path of self-destruction or if you want to make the change. People will judge you for wanting to be better, for wanting a change, for wanting more than what you have in this moment. It will appear as if you think you are better than, or smarter than, but those opinions should not have the power to stop you from moving forward. You are allowed to have boundaries and be unapologetic for it.

Here is the good news; I did not break! I fought like hell to dig myself out of the hole I was left in. And you can too. My hope is that my story will help you too.

"Shame dies when your story is told in a safe place." – Ann Voskamp

CHAPTER 3
Why I Stayed

How could someone you love so unconditionally hurt you to your core and try to break your spirit? I assume, since you are reading this, that you also have the strength within you to thrive. You are not to be broken. Brokenhearted, hurt, our self-worth diminished, rumors being said, self-esteem questionable. Yes, all those things, but *never truly broken*. I was hurt to my core! I never thought I would be hurt as badly as I was. The hurt was so intense I experienced physical pain. I did not eat, I hardly slept, and I did not want connection with anyone. I knew there was potential for violence and abuse because I had experienced the abuse for many years, but this extreme act was a shock. The only logical reasoning I could accept was this was the last attempt at making me so fearful that I would never leave permanently. I had the ability to manage and over-come all forms of abuse, because it was familiar to me, but nobody should ever have to deal with abuse.

People ask me why I stayed. Does it really make a difference why someone stays? I do not think so, but I stayed because I genuinely was in love. I stayed because I thought I could out love the past hurt and pain. I stayed because I was afraid of the changes that would occur. I stayed because I did not want to know what life would be like without the intense love.

Have you ever been so fearful of someone that you stayed to survive? You stayed to keep yourself or your loved ones safe? You stayed to keep the image, to keep the peace? You did not have access to finances, or you did not have a place to go? Maybe you were like me, and you did not want your kids to grow up in a broken home. Or you heard a saying as I did. It is safer to be in bed with the devil than not know where the devil is. Something bad, but something you know, is better than the unknown. I did not leave because of all these things I had listed. Making sense of something that makes no sense to you is a losing battle. You will never figure out their why.

> *You might not be able to distinguish which pain was worse, the shock of what happened, or the ache for what never will.* —author unknown

It does not matter what your reason is for staying. What matters is that you know. That you acknowledge why you did. It does not have to make sense to anyone else. People who have been through the trauma, do not need a justification.

People would ask me if I still loved him, or if I hated him. To which I would answer no! For me to love or hate, would mean that I must care. After the amount of work that I had done, it did not serve a purpose for me to care anymore. I said farewell to all of it and left it in the past and closed that chapter of my story. Closing that chapter did not mean it never happened, it meant I was finally free from it. It meant that closing that chapter of my life, allowed me to move into the next chapter. I was able to see all the blessings that were placed in front of me and be grateful for them.

If you are in a shitty situation or relationship, do you feel obligated to stay? If so, why?

_____

_____

_____

CHAPTER 4
Grief

I will mention the suicide of my youngest brother throughout this book. I have never in my life experienced something so physically, mentally, and emotionally debilitating. It completely ripped my soul from my chest and wrecked me. I had just talked to my brother a couple of hours before I got the call. When I heard my mom's god-awful screech and screaming on the phone, I froze. I panicked. My neighbor found me screaming in my driveway, braless. In those moments I had feelings of shock and disbelief. I was overwhelmed, and I had lots of guilt. Much of it was a blur. I was not able to function enough to drive so my neighbors drove me to my brother's house.

I made all the phone calls that needed to be made. At that time, I was the only other sibling who was in the state. And honestly, I felt like such an asshole because I was the one who had to call and give people the shitty news. I remember the officer at the scene saying, "I was told that you were the one who is going to hold it all together." And I did. But at that time, I did not know what I needed, so I put my energy into taking care of everyone else and making sure everyone else was okay. I buried what I had to, in the attempt to provide comfort to them.

This is what I knew how to do, and it played a major role in my becoming a complete shit show. I hid the emotions I was having, or rather suppressed them. I did not want to deal with those hard feelings. I had no idea how to manage those feelings when I had not dealt with my emotions from the prior trauma with my toxic person. It is the most extreme painful situation imaginable. It is just as bad as you would imagine. Worse than you would have imagined. You must get to a place where you are able to acknowledge the pain you are feeling.

Honestly, I do not think grief is visible on us from the outside. Maybe to the people who are extra close to you and can read what you are saying without saying anything. But the people who do not have close access to you do not know what grief has done to you. Healing from grief means you must get to a place where you accept there is never going to be a solution to the pain you carry. It is not something that needs to be figured out.

I was always super annoyed with people who told me, "It will get better." I know their comments came from a good place, but all I would say is "When? When does it get better?" You will need people in your life to just hold your hand, and offer support because honestly you don't even know what you are needing in those moments, so how are you supposed to ask for something you do not know you need?

Something you must understand is grief is not just something you deal with in the death of a loved one. It is something you must also deal with when you lose a relationship, a job, or a picture you have painted in your head of a family. Losing any of those things needs to be grieved. I did not understand that because I did not know it played a significant role of how I was viewing things. If you think about it this way, maybe you were with your partner for many years, and the relationship ends. That is an extreme loss. The loss of that partner, the loss of the life you had built together, family time together, family trips, experiencing the children's first things if you have children together, the memories you had made, the future you had made, the in-laws if you have a good relationship with them—all those things are losses.

Grief is like a house in flames. I use this analogy because I have had this happen to a home. But what I mean is a little flicker of fire can cause so much chaos. It is like a little fire, and just the right airflow will start the next thing on fire, and the next. Soon, the house is filled with smoke, then the fire is gaining momentum and the whole house is up in flames. Just like emotions with grief. One moment you might be feeling a little sad, and that is manageable; then maybe a song comes on that reminds you of them, and you start to cry. Then you see their picture, and your breathing becomes faster. Soon your mind is filled with chaos because your emotions have taken over, and you cannot stop them from coming. Then you find yourself in fetal position on the floor or wrapped up in your blankets choking, and you honestly do not feel like the pain will ever stop. And then the music is blaring a song that makes your cry even harder. Your nose becomes plugged, and your head is pounding, the intensity is top notch, and the pounding will not stop.

In those moments, you will not want to feel how you are feeling because it is too much to bear. Those feelings are real and okay to have. It is okay to be like "Fuck you, Porter" (that is my brother's name); it is okay to be angry at thar person or the people you have lost. It is okay to be mad. You may feel like parts of your life were stolen from you, and that is okay. If that is how you feel, it is valid. Do not let someone tell that how you are feeling is not valid. I am here to tell you your feelings are valid.

The death of my brother had me in over my head. I was remarkably close to my brother; I was his second mom. I spent time with Porter quite often. Porter made shitty decisions, but that did not change the amount of love that I still have in my heart that I want to give to him. We all make shitty decisions that will impact you in one way or another, but you are still worthy or love.

Most people say, "Just get over it; just move on." But in all reality, it does not work that way. You cannot just get over or move on from things like this. You must work *through* them. Let the emotions come! I know this sounds silly, but let your body feel what it needs to feel. It will help you heal. You do not have to live in those emotions forever or even for a long time, but you do have to acknowledge them and make them valid. It is a part of who you are in those moments.

It is okay if this happens over and over or for days or weeks in a row. It is okay to not be okay. It is okay to think you are completely fine one day, and then you become a shit show, and you are crying and do not even know why you are crying. Let yourself feel. I know this can be hard because if you are like me, you learned to suppress what you were feeling. Your feelings might not have been validated, or you were made fun of because you were crying or told that you were weak because you were crying. Crying is not a sign of weakness. It takes much more strength to acknowledge the emotions than to suppress them. The reality is you will grieve forever. You will not get over the loss of a loved one; you will learn to live with it. You will heal and rebuild yourself around the loss you have suffered. You will be whole again, but you will never be the same. Nor should you be the same, nor would you want to be.

Grief is crippling. Every day you wake up, you do everything you can to make sure everyone else is okay. We do everything for everyone else and forget about ourselves. This can also be used as a distraction. Emotions of grief come in waves, some days they crush me, and some days they show me that he is near and watching over me, but the pain never goes away.

After my brother committed suicide, I started spiraling downward. I have been through some real-life shit, like explosive diarrhea shit. But despite all those horrible things I had dealt with, those events did not break me. Those events made me want to keep fighting harder.

After I had gone through a lifetime of hurt and destruction, I managed all those things that happened to me. I managed the assault and the torment. I was not going to let anyone destroy me. I still lived every day with hope and love. I was accepting of what had happened to me. Those things that happened to me did not define me. In my mind, I could overcome anything.

But the kicker, the death of me, was my brother's suicide. The loss of him, wrecked me worse than anything that had ever been done to me, in my entire life. After I lost my brother, I felt depleted and defeated. Everything in my soul was shattered. My whole being was at war within itself. My mind thought it was right, but my heart thought it was wrong. It was a never-ending war within me. I became destructive to myself. I was completely lost.

I had become withdrawn and shut my emotions down. I was neglecting myself, and I had no boundaries. I will also discuss boundaries in chapter twelve. At this point, I did not know how to implement them. I wanted to feel present, but I needed to take care of everyone else. I recognize now, I did not have the tools to provide myself with what I needed. I came to terms with the fact that I was lost without my brother; he was a significant part of who I am.

With him, I could express true laughter and genuine happiness. With him, I knew pure love and joy. His softness still resonates within me. After I lost my brother, my world stopped. I was angry that everyone else's went on. I was jealous that, in a sense, they were able to move forward without feeling the intense pain that I was feeling. I was starving myself of happiness. I felt that, if I was happy, I was forgetting about my brother.

Have you ever had to grieve the loss of someone or something? What was that like for you?

_____
_____
_____
_____

If you have, how has it shaped you?

_____
_____
_____
_____

CHAPTER 5
Vindictiveness toward Yourself

First, what is vindictiveness? In my experience, and the work I have done on myself, I would say it is all the negative things that you tell yourself about yourself—things like "I am not good enough, not smart enough;" "I am ugly, my legs are too big." Basically, insulting yourself to the point you believe it. I had been vindictive to myself by telling myself I was stupid for staying in an unhealthy relationship, or I was at fault because I "let" those things happen. I held myself responsible for things that were out of my control.

What role did it play in my journey? I was vindictive to myself by labeling myself the outcast. I did not realize it at the time, but I did this to justify how I was. I was withdrawn and awkward; I gave people the cold shoulder. I was very observant of others. I did not feel I could relate to those around me. I did not want to start the conversations for fear of a conversation coming up about things that had happened to me or being asked how things were going.

I learned the choices for my life were my responsibility. How I respond to criticism, how I behave toward others, and the expectations I have are all my responsibility. I had to be willing to kill parts of myself so I could grow something new. I needed to be willing to rebuild parts of myself that were already within me. It did not mean I had to forget who I was in those moments, but I had to have the desire to want something better for myself.

Have you ever asked yourself why you behave or react the way you do? Have you ever wondered if it is more a safety tactic and a defense mechanism to keep you safe, than it is how you truly are? I had some time to reflect and learned I was taught to react inadvertently.

Do you wonder if there are other parts that play a role in your behavior? Does vindictiveness play a role in your life? Let us be honest for a minute. Are you anything like me? Do you shut down, avoid, redirect, or use humor when things become difficult?

_____

_____

_____

_____

Let me ask you this What are some of the challenges that you are facing right now, in this moment? What strengths do you possess to overcome challenges?

_____

_____

_____

_____

I am optimistic, I try to find the good in every situation, I find ways to make any situation work, and I can adapt to change quickly.

Are you willing to push yourself past your triggers? Are you willing to try your hardest to keep pushing forward when you feel yourself shutting down? Are you willing to pull yourself back into that part of yourself you are trying to avoid?

For this book to be beneficial and helpful to you, you must be honest with yourself. If you are trying to hide from yourself or withholding information from yourself, you are limiting the amount of helpful information you can learn.

There will be times in your life or your journey where you will feel people are being inconsiderate of your feelings or your triggers. Honestly, some of those people are being intentional, but most often it is likely that another person's offense toward you is not intentional. In any of these situations though, make no mistake, the situation will cause you to display or feel very intense emotions or reactions such as being judgmental or ashamed, shifting blame, or denial. All of these are valid.

You must also understand that what you are feeling has everything to do with you and your response.

My goal is to help you find clarity and help you obtain some hope to let your past experiences surface. To process the things that have been suppressed. Peeling the layers of yourself back so you have a better understanding of who you truly are meant to be.

CHAPTER 6

How I View Myself: Why It Matters

Growing up, I matured at an incredibly early age. By the time I was in third grade I had already gotten my period. By the time I was in sixth grade, I was at my peak height. I am still a solid five-three; I have not gotten any taller since. I was bullied in elementary; I was bigger and taller than the other kids. I was called fat and ugly in second grade. I developed a complex about myself at an immature age. I thought of myself as the ugly duckling. I was insecure. I never felt like I fit in anywhere, I was socially awkward, and I felt out of place all the time.

By the time I started junior high, my beauty had started to appear, and I still felt out of place. Girls would comment about my ass, which I think now is my greatest asset. Girls were mean to me. I did not have many female friends. However, I was able to turn the negative comments about my figure into something positive.

Looking back, I wonder if I was misunderstood by others. My own insecurities caused me to give the cold shoulder and come off stuck-up or conceited because I was insecure about not fitting in. Throughout your life, many people will play a role in your life. Either they will enhance your insecurities, or they will prove the insecurities to be untrue. People who played a role in your childhood were acting out their own insecurities about themselves. Maybe it was not about jealousy; maybe it was about wishing you were like someone and could not be, so people were mean.

I have learned the way that I viewed myself plays a part in who I am today. Those annoying comments or mean behaviors haunted me—until I accepted them for what they were: irrelevant.

I always thought that things like my trauma would never happen to me. I was in a small town; everyone knew "of" everyone. I purposely said "of" someone because most people only knew of me because of my last name, or they know "of" me based on stories they have heard about me from someone else who also did not know me. Most often the people talking about me never truly knew me.

Most people do not have close access to me, and I do this with purpose. I like to call the people who always had something to say about me "flying monkeys" because this is the best term that I have been exposed to throughout my journey. If you do not know what flying monkeys are, they are people who actively engage in a smear campaign with the toxic person. They tried ridiculously hard to destroy my reputation. Their actions say more about them than it does about me. I do admit it can be hurtful, shameful, and embarrassing. I did not understand why someone would want to be a pawn in someone's game, but I do recognize now, but these people who were apart of trying to torment me have not evolved or grown within themselves for years.

I also understand now there are people who will try to gather information about your situations so there is more to gossip about. You will have people in your life, maybe not those with direct access to you, who watch your every move so there is something to gossip about. These people will always exist. These people will always have something to say about what they *think* is going on in your life. It is most likely lies, rumors, gossip, and deceit.

The best thing I learned is to let them. You must be confident enough in yourself and your choices that opinions and rumors are something to giggle at, because let's face it: most people who have never experienced extreme trauma or loss have never done the work you are doing. Besides, I now enjoy hearing rumors about myself. It is quite comical. I have evolved tremendously throughout my journey that when I hear things about myself or things about my life, I tell people to run with what they think they know and have a party.

To be completely transparent, I have an extremely low tolerance for people who talk about things they know nothing about, people who are ignorant, people who have a negative mindset, and people who always feel the need to talk about someone else.

> *The purpose of gossip is to manipulate the narrative, the second you hear gossip, you should know who got it twisted.* —Kalen Dion

Growing up, I was exposed to sexuality. I remember seeing paintings of the most beautiful Native American women, with the long hair and perfect bodies. I am part Native American, so maybe I am biased when it comes to Native American beauty. I can appreciate a women's beauty. I like to give women compliments about things that I appreciate. But nonetheless, I recognize now that I developed an insecurity about the way I looked because I was not made to have the body of those beautiful Native women to which I was exposed. I was thicker than a snicker, I still am and proud to be. Whatever type of complex you have about yourself will play a significant role in situations you find yourself in.

My point is this: as you get older and learn more about yourself, rumors and gossip will have less of an impact on you. Eventually you will be secure enough in yourself people's opinion will not make a difference in your view of yourself. You will learn you are enough, and you are worthy of being treated with respect. The things you tell yourself, such as negative thoughts about yourself, are what your brain will make you believe. So, stop talking shit to yourself.

Do not waste your time trying to entertain a discussion or argument with anybody who does not have the knowledge and/or experience of things you have gone through. Honestly, they most likely do not care about your truth or what is honest; they are focused only on what their own beliefs are. Never waste your time and energy on discussions that make no sense to you.

You can present all the evidence you have, present everything that supports your claim, but there will always be people who neither possess the ability to understand nor care to understand. They are blind to anything being different than what they believe to be true; they are driven by hate, pride, and their own ego, and their own resentment, which has nothing to do with you.

Take a moment to think back to your childhood? Were there some things that you were subjected to or exposed to that had an impact on your view of yourself today? Jot them down.

_____

_____

_____

_____

Try not to overthink it; just try to write whatever comes to mind. It might not make sense in this moment, but you will gain some clarity eventually. Writing things down will give you an idea of areas you need to address—things that may still have a hold on you of which you are unaware. For me, I did not realize the impact of being exposed to the beautiful naked women and the way it affected the view I had of myself. Do you have a negative complex about yourself? If so, where did it come from?

_____

_____

_____

_____

Heal so you do not have underlying issues when trying to have a conversation with someone else. Heal so you do not take your own frustration out on others or those close to you. Heal so when someone compliments you or expresses their love for you, you can believe what is being said to you.

This is a little side not for you to get to know a little more about me. I can be very persistent. I function best under pressure; I can be reckless at times and tend to be impulsive. I also know that I am very stubborn and headstrong. I do not listen to people's advice; I would rather do things on my own and most often find things out the hard way.

If I want something, I make it happen. I have trained my mind to become extraordinarily strong. When I get angry, I cry. I do not lash out or react in an aggressive way, I cry. I love extremely hard, and I will give someone the shirt off my back if they need it. I have the belief that there is always someone else who has it worse than I do or did. I tend to be extremely optimistic and can find the best in every single situation. I can learn something from every single situation.

How do you manage anger? Are you quick to react? Brush things under the rug? Take a minute to be honest with yourself.

_____

_____

_____

_____

Let them say what they want and stand firm in your truth. —*author unknown*

CHAPTER 7
Distractions: Not Denial

To get to the point of facing your trauma, you must face your distractions. Let us talk about distractions! You must understand at this point you are suffering from a lot of internal chaos. It is extremely easy to be in denial at this point, at least it was for me. Distractions are a blessing and a curse to be honest. After my brother committed suicide, I lost my shit. One of the most important people in my life was never coming back. My world fell apart. I knew my mind was falling apart and my heart was shattered!

I was at war within myself. I still was a mother, and I took care and supported the children, and I worked, but I was numb. I was furious with my brother. I told you I would mention him a lot in this book. I felt like he had abandoned me when I needed him the most. My brother was like my own child, so it was extremely hard for me to even try to navigate the emotions I was feeling. I found myself finding distractions—whether it was social media, working out, drinking, stress cleaning, gambling, taking on things that I did not want to do, going places I did not want to go, or being around people I did not want to be around. There are so many things that are readily available to be used as a distraction. I found distractions so I did not have to face my own reality. You will find yourself doing things that do not connect with your core values. You will act out of character, different than who you truly are. You will not be your best self because finding that person means you must deal with the hurt and heartache and work through the obstacles.

You will not realize what your distractions are until after they are not a distraction anymore. More like until you have found yourself running in the opposite directions for a significant amount of time. They filled the void I felt of missing my brother. When I met someone who allowed me to feel closer to my brother, we spent a lot of time together. We went on vacations together and spent holidays together. I was in love with his personality and his character. We were drawn to each other; our chemistry was incredible. This too was a distraction.

Distractions are easy to do. They supply a sense of security when things are falling apart. They supply stability when you need it. You will use it to make it to the next day or to deal with the next disappointment. What I later learned was all my mixed-up emotions were grief. Let me just say that grief almost destroyed me, and I talked about grief in chapter four.

Distractions are a very passive coping mechanism. Distractions helped me cope without having to deal with the issue. Distractions initially worked to help me take away intense feelings I was dealing with but did not help me long-term. I knew I could not outrun the intense emotions I was having and one day I would have to face them. But for the time being, I used distractions to keep me sane. The distractions kept me safe in the moment and allowed me moments where I could regulate my emotions short-term. I felt like a complete crazy person after I lost my brother.

People who are diagnosed with anxiety and post-traumatic stress disorder, like I am, my brain overstimulated for me to cope, so using distractions helped my brain slow down. Distractions are like unhealthy coping mechanisms. I numbed myself to not have to feel what I was feeling. I used them to keep myself exceptionally busy. I was always doing something. Doing so allowed me to keep my focus on things that did not have anything to do with my hurt, trauma, or loss.

It is quite easy to fall into this cycle. It took me a long time to realize that I was doing these things to avoid dealing with my shit. I did not want to feel the hurt or deal with the emotion. I wanted to suppress it and pretend that it did not exist. This is an unbelievably bad idea! When all my shit came to surface, I was a train wreck. Remember earlier when I told you I was a complete shit show with broken blood vessels in my eyes. That is what I am referring to. Distractions are always going to be there. You must decide when enough is enough and take control of your life

    What are some of your distractions? What kind of comfort do they support you?

_____

_____

_____

_____

CHAPTER 8
Downward Spiral

I was sitting in my car after an appointment with my plastic surgeon, drowning in hurt, anger, sorrow, uncertainty, and despair. I called my mom, completely distraught. I am spouting off at the mouth. I do not want to live like this anymore; I do not want to feel the way I am feeling. I feel lost and alone and like nobody understands. What is happening to me? How did I become this person? I need to go to intensive therapy or something. I hate what I have been through. I wish this had not happened to me. I felt like there was no way out, nowhere else to turn. I felt like nobody could understand how I was feeling in that moment. I felt defenseless. I felt withdrawn. I felt numb. I felt anxious and confused.

Tears are rolling down my face, and I am completely beside myself. I feel completely defeated in that moment. My contacts are blurry, my nose is all full of boogers, and I am a mess!

Someone I love shows up, and he sees the darkness in my eyes. I am blank. I had given up hope. "You didn't see the darkness in her eyes," he says; "she isn't okay." We sat in my car in the parking lot and were calling and researching intensive therapy options, we called the suicide hotline number, we called suicide prevention centers, and I texted my therapist and let her know I needed to be seen immediately. I even considered committing myself for a 72 hour hold somewhere. I could not physically handle the pain any longer.

Have you ever felt so low in your life that you wanted to give up? You did not want to die or commit suicide, but you just wanted the pain to go away? Because I have. I just wanted the pain to stop; I wanted to hurt to go away. I desperately wanted to feel "normal." When is the last time that you have had these feelings? They were recent, they were months ago or years ago, but they have not fully gone away. You do not have to write anything down, but I ask you to just take a moment to think about that for a minute. How are you feeling right now?

_____

_____

_____

_____

I went to therapy the day after my meltdown, unaware that day would change my life forever. I am telling my therapist what is going on in my mind, and I feel like I am talking a hundred miles a minute. Nothing is making sense to me. Everything is completely coming out of my mouth from all angles. Complete mental tension, my anxiety has taken over. My thoughts run faster than my mouth can speak. I am not sure if I should be crying or laughing, I do not know what is up or down. I am all over the place.

Have you ever experienced this? I knew something was not right with me, but I could not figure out what it was. I was scared; I had never felt so desperate in my life. I learned quickly that desperation will make a person do things that are not of normal character.

We looked up some places that I could go for an intensive therapy. I was feeling extremely anxious, overwhelmed, and my patience had dwindled to nothing.

I called this retreat center, and I desperately knew I needed to go to this place. During this time, I had lost my sense of who I was and my confidence in making my own decisions. I was made to believe that I was not smart enough to make my own choices. I tended to get another thought on my own thinking to decide if my thought was sufficient. I was made to believe that I did not have the qualities to make my own decisions.

I made an impulsive decision and put down the deposit that same day. This decision was a life changer. It turned out to be the most incredible, horrifying, beautiful, and awful experience of my life. Not only did I deal with my own shit, but I learned the reasons behind how I got to the place I was at in my life, why I was second-guessing everything, and how to retake control over myself and my life.

CHAPTER 9
The Process

I have spent these last month's solely focusing on myself and the children. It has been incredible. Earlier in the book, I talked about when I was a shit show, and I really thought everything had fallen apart and I had hit rock bottom, back in Chapter Five. You know when I was sitting in my car after my appointment with my plastic surgeon? I was going to the Hoffman Process. A six-night, seven-day intensive trauma healing retreat center in Petaluma, California. I was terrified to go, but more fearful of what condition I would be in if I did not go. I thought about taking the loss of money that was invested into this place, but I did not.

My therapist was in contact with my coach and had to be available for communication in case there was something going on with me in which they could not help. The coaches are also therapists. My therapist had to give permission that I was in the right place in my healing and that I was ready for this because, little did I know, this was going to be harder than anything I had ever done in my life.

In one of my therapy sessions a couple of days before I left for the Process, I had a conversation with my therapist, and she said, "There will come a point during this process when you are going to want to leave." My dumb ass rolled my eyes, like she was bat shit crazy. That woman was not lying. I promised myself I would not leave, no matter what happened.

I was assigned to a coach prior to going, and this coach was aware of my situation and the obstacles I was facing prior to going, due to the required homework. Homework was needed to get your mind and body ready for the Process. I do not think I have ever been as honest with myself as I was with the homework. I mentioned negative patterns earlier in the book, and I had lots of them. I can give an example that might make sense: when I feel like I am being unheard, I shut down my emotions and I am withdrawn. So, when something does not sit right with me, I react with something. If I am being yelled at, I tune out and hear nothing. I learned my reasonings behind why I react to things the way I do and where I learned it.

I arrived on Friday night, the night before the Process started, and already I was like "What the hell did I commit to?" By the next morning, we jumped right in. There was no easing into it. We started the Process, and we were doing an exercise. I had not yet worked through the trauma on when I was physically and sexually assaulted with my therapist. I was more focused on taking care of everyone else. This exercise felt like I was hit by the biggest waves of the ocean and being knocked down by them repeatedly. I felt like I was drowning. Holy shit, the exercise nearly broke me. During the exercise it was as if the past three years of my life came rushing out, and let me just say, there was no way to stop it from happening. I took a huge emotional beating from the exercise.

After that exercise, my coach came and checked on me, and I was very vague. I said something like "I am good." I minimized the effect this exercise had because I knew what was going to happen if I admitted how I was really feeling. I went out to the bench, and I started crying. And in my mind, I was thinking, *you are not okay, you are not okay.* My body instantly went to flight mode. Think back to when I mentioned this in Chapter 7. I rushed back inside, found my coach, and said, "I am not okay. I want to leave, but I had a car service bring me here." I am looking around the room and looking for all the exits in case I need to run. My body is in survival mode, by default, because my brain was sensing danger based on the emotions I was experiencing—the same emotions I had during the actual trauma. However, I was not in danger. In fact, I was in the safest place I could have been.

A safe place is somewhere that you can break down your emotions and talk about them without fear of getting in trouble or having to deal with any consequences. There is no actual threat to danger.

Earlier in my discussion with my coach when she was assigned to me, I also told her to not let me leave, no matter what. My coach was incredible. Not to say that the other three coaches were not incredible also, but she was my coach, so we spent more time together. My coach put her hands on my shoulders and reassured me that I was in no real danger. We got me back to a sense of safety, and I went back to my seat. I sat with my extreme emotions, something I had never experienced before. Not that I have not ever had extreme emotions, but I have never had the complete safe space to be able to sit with them and reflect on them. The Process is not easy; it is extremely hard.

During one of the classes, they asked everyone what we were fighting for. With no hesitation or fear of being judged, I said, "My life." I was fighting for my life. I did not know until that moment I was coming out of this experience as a victor. I sat with my emotions for hours. We went right into another exercise that had everything to do with the exercise before, and I had nothing. I was not mad, sad, or angry, but I was confused. I asked myself, *why are you not reacting right now?* So of course, I must be doing something wrong, because everyone else was doing the exercise.

I found one of the other coaches and I asked him why I was not reacting the way I assumed I should be, and he said, "Do you not realize what you just did? Do you understand that you just sat with your emotions and processed them? What you just did was extremely hard. You sat with your emotions, you felt your emotions, and you embraced them and let them go." I asked him if I should be trying to provoke other emotions to come out, and he said, "No, you did the hard work." Saying hard work sounds silly, but doing the hard work is having the courage to face what is haunting you.

The Process is designed in such an intent way that does not make any sense until after the Process is done. My layers were peeled back as they needed to be, but not one at a time. I do not want to say too much else about this Process in case someone else decides to undergo it. I would not want to take anything away from the experience it offers. It does cost a good chunk of money, but it is an amazing investment in yourself. I dealt with things from my earliest childhood to the present day. I learned about things that I was mad about that I did not know I was mad about. If you ever get the opportunity to go to the Hoffman Process, I highly recommend doing it. It does not have to be the Hoffman Process, but any intensive retreat program. It was not until I completed this program, did the reflection, and came back home that I understood what I was doing wrong—and not only what I was doing wrong, but why I was doing it wrong, and how to change it.

The other thing that played a significant part of being able to start healing from the loss of my brother was commonalities based around the Process. All I saw was my brother. Everything about this place and the temperament and kindness was like I had experienced with my brother. I felt peace. I knew right then that my brother was telling me it was okay to heal. It was okay to embrace the pain. He was telling me that he did not want me to carry the burdens he carried any longer and it was time to let myself heal.

A little side note: antlers signify my brother for me. When I arrived at the Process, the first thing I saw was a buck. I am a firm believer that everything happens for a reason; it might be a shitty reason, but nonetheless it will serve a purpose and give a lesson. For me, it was time to let my guilt and shame go. It was time for me to love myself for loving my brother, for loving my trauma and experiences. It was time to take it easy on myself because I am not made of stone.

Have you had the opportunity to do any kind of reflection or the opportunity to go to a retreat? If so, what did you learn?

_____

_____

_____

_____

_____

CHAPTER 10
How Others Viewed Me

I often wonder what kind of impression I give to people who look at me. Do I give off an inviting vibe, a calm vibe, an accepting vibe? Do I seem stuck up? Unapproachable? I feel like I have a resting bitch face, and most of the time I do not engage with people.

> *Ignorance can be very loud, and that is usually when the intelligent ones become quiet. It never serves a purpose to plead your case when nobody is willing to listen or be open minded. —author unknown*

I have taken the plunge and asked some of my closest people what their first impressions were of me. Bold move, right? Or dumb, and I will be really upset about what they say, right? I was overjoyed with the amount of genuine feedback I got. Here is what I have gathered from this group of incredible people.

These are the people that I met when I went to the Process, something I discussed in the earlier chapter. These incredible people met me at my lowest, and I said goodbye at my best.

- "The first time I met you, I felt a little bit of guarded energy, but I also knew that there was something else going on." Her instinct was I was holding back but with real reason. She said, "Do not discount the fact that initial impressions are based on ways we have learned how to protect ourselves based on our actual experiences." Once she was able to get though the initial feelings of a wall, there was something special and strong there.
- "You appeared to be intimidating. Like someone who would not like me because of how I appear or speak. When we had to do that exercise together, and I looked into your eyes, I could see the soft, kindhearted spirit in those big, beautiful doe eyes you have, but also that you are a survivor of something serious, like you are tough because you must be, with major underlying reason and serious pain and vulnerability."
- "We had an exercise where you felt I was trying to 'see you' and ask deep questions early on, and I try to connect with people, but with you it was tricky. I felt you were

guarded and keeping your distance. I was curious why and kept trying."
- "I try to make friends with everyone, but you are more selective on who you let in your life."

What I have learned from this is that first impressions are usually bullshit. First impressions are usually very judgmental. They can come from a place of insecurity of the person making the assumptions. People tend to assume everyone else has their shit together while they are personally going through a challenging time. Many people do not do the challenging work you are doing and face their own shame and demons and aren't able to acknowledge their own imperfections to themselves, let alone to others.

I recently reached out to someone from many years ago, and I simply apologized to her for something I thought I had done to her and said I was sorry if I had made her feel insecure or unloved. When I was writing the message, I was genuinely sorry if I had hurt her. I did not need a response and was not expecting one. When I got a message back within seconds, it was unexpected. What was most surprising to me was it was a very defensive response on her part.

I now understand if you are apologizing and you have done your work, but the other person cannot receive the apology, then most likely they have not put in the hard work on themselves. I learned it is not that you are unlikable. It is that if you do not play the role in which they have cast you in their mind, then how can they play the role they want to play in their own mind? I learned that responses such as this have nothing to do with me.

Allowing someone to create a false narrative of you is a small price to pay for having rid yourself of their toxicity. – Author Unknown

Statements like this helped me put words to how I portray myself. I come off very distant because I am selective. One of them trying to "see" me made me close off even more because I did not want them to see that I was struggling at my core or that I was intimidating, which is never my goal but more of a defense mechanism. All these statements from people who have met me and know me made it easier for me to understand how people are viewing me, and I am more able to find why I am doing those things.

Our initial experience of a person can also have a lot to do with our own insecurities or battles that we are facing. It matters what you think about yourself. It matters because without even knowing it, that is how you are presenting yourself for others to see. You can either be your own biggest cheerleader or your own worst enemy. Everything you feed yourself impacts every part of yourself. The more you think negatively about yourself, the more limitations you are setting up for yourself.

You must understand this: the negative beliefs that you have about yourself are not your true self. Those negative thoughts are your subconscious thoughts and are not your own. Subconscious thoughts can be hard to recognize. I read in an article that subconscious thoughts come from a place in the mind that are not in current awareness. Subconscious thoughts affect many parts of our being. These negative characteristics have been told to you throughout your whole life since childhood. But the good news is there is a way to get out from under these thoughts and stop letting yourself believe the lies. Acknowledgment and self-affirmation, in my experience, are the key. Try making post-its and sticking them on your mirror, with positive affirmations such as "I am enough, I am strong, I am kind, I am worthy, and I am lovable." Talk to yourself in the mirror; journal all the good things about yourself. Being consistent with these affirmations will train your brain to believe what you are telling it. I know from experience this is a very shitty, hard, and exhausting place to be in.

Take a minute to jot down your thoughts about yourself: things such as beliefs about yourself. For example, at the beginning of my journey, I would have said things like "I am not good enough, I am not lovable, I am at fault, I should have been better, I should have tried harder, I should have been more aware, and I am not pretty enough." Thoughts about myself now that I have put distance between the trauma and my healing: "I am courageous, I am bold, I am worthy, I am lovable, I am kind, I am giving, I am genuine." List a few things about yourself, no matter what part of your journey you are on.

_____
_____
_____
_____

What are some of your insecurities?

_____
_____
_____
_____
_____

What are some of your best assets?

_____
_____
_____
_____

CHAPTER 11
It Is All about You

This healing process has nothing to do with any other people involved in your trauma or loss. Absolutely nothing. At first it is all about them, the things they did, and how they wronged you. You may want answers like I did, or closure. People involved have *zero* things to do with your healing. It is all about *you*. It will be all the effort you put into trying to heal. It will be about you being vulnerable with yourself and being honest with your therapist if you have one. It will be you being honest about your own flaws and the questionable choices you may have made—figuring out why you were in certain situations or what led you to be there.

You must understand I did not truly start to heal until I found the right therapist, and most importantly, I went *no contact* with anything and anyone that was detrimental to my healing. I will explain later in chapter thirteen why this was important and helpful to me.

Everyone loves therapy. I mean everyone. Just kidding. I hated it at first too. Do you have the same issue I did? I was very skeptical about going to therapy. Not because I did not want the help, not because I was scared to, but because I did not want someone trying to counsel me with only knowledge from reading a book. I knew I needed someone who had gone through and overcome some real-life experiences, some real-life hardships. I am not saying this is a bad choice, but I know myself enough to know I needed a certain type of therapist to help me on my journey to healing.

I needed someone who could put words and definitions to things I was experiencing. I needed someone who was not going to sugarcoat anything for me, someone who was not going to feed me bullshit, someone who was just as blunt as I was, but also someone who could meet me where I was at in my level of healing. I needed someone who was not afraid to drop the F bomb. Someone who would challenge me. Someone who would question the statements I made and make me ponder on my reasonings. I needed someone who would offer grace and insight. Someone who would help guide me to find the answers to my problem instead of just telling me an answer or fixing the problem for me. I had three therapists prior to finding the one I have been with for a couple of years now, and I have complete trust in her and thank God, I found her.

What are some qualities you need in a therapist if you are searching for one? Or on the other side, if you already have a therapist, what are some qualities you admire about them?

_____

_____

_____

_____

Healing takes patience and compassion for yourself, forgiveness of yourself, and awareness of yourself. Allow grace for yourself, because you will take steps backward, you will make mistakes, and mess up. Most importantly, be intentional of what you want the result to be, the goal toward which you are working. Healing means being able to cry in therapy or alone in your room or screaming in the car with blood vessels in your eyes breaking. That was me, a complete shit show. But there's beauty in it; it is an always changing shit show, depending on the effort you are putting in.

I am here right now, authoring my story in the hopes your journey might be a little easier than mine was. In the hopes you can be open, honest, and vulnerable enough and hopefully meet you where you are at in your journey. Maybe you are just starting out in your journey. Maybe you are months in or years in. Wherever you are in your journey, I understand. I have been there. And it takes an extreme amount of demanding work, but you are strong enough to make it.

I was taking many steps backward. I would go to therapy weeks at a time, and I did not realize it at the time, but now I realize I was going to therapy upset over the same thing I was upset about the week prior. I was not changing what I was doing. It was the same conversation, the same things I could change, but I was not making the intentional choice to make the change I needed. I was making excuses for myself; I was not being honest with myself about what was happening to me. I was justifying everything that had been done to me and justifying why I was at fault for my loss and trauma.

Are you experiencing something similar? Are you in denial? Are you justifying actions toward you? More important, is it making a difference?

_____

_____

_____

_____

I had lots of things I needed to work on about myself. All types of negative patterns. I briefly discussed this in chapter nine.

I am not perfect, nor do I seek perfection, but only to have a better understanding of myself.

Once I learned that a person's behavior toward me had nothing to do with me, things got much easier for me to make sense of. It was incredibly hard for me to navigate not only my own emotions but the emotions of four children. Let me tell you getting to know yourself is hard. There is a lot of denial, there is a lot of hesitation, and there is a lot of confusion. It is extremely hard to know who you really are and to decide what your core values are when your mind is running on overload—when you are constantly being told that this or that is wrong or trying to do things in a manner that will not cause chaos.

Are you at a point in your life where you are grateful for the things that you have experienced? I do not mean that you are happy they happened to you, or you deserved anything you have experienced. I mean can you give your experience and, most important, your arduous work some credit for forming you into the person you are now? I do not mean the way people say shitty situations make you stronger, because they do not. You made yourself stronger. The trauma or loss did not make you stronger.

Do not ever let anything else take any credit for you becoming the best version of yourself. I do not assume that you would ever wish your story on someone else, because it is horrible, but I do know for certain that when you work through your story, you will be grateful for parts of it and what it has taught you.

You made the choice to pick up this book and read it. You made the choice to try to gather information. You made the choice to say "No"," or leave. You are making the choices for yourself in these moments. I am proud of you!

Think about what lessons you have learned throughout your journey. Have they made a major impact on your life right now?

_____

_____

_____

_____

Why are you grateful? What have you learned about yourself? Maybe you are grateful that you are more open-minded, or kinder or more aware that everyone is going through something.

_____

_____

_____

_____

I learned how to verbalize my emotions and articulate why I was feeling the way I was feeling. I learned how to listen and try to understand, instead of thinking about what I am going to say next. I learned to listen to my instincts.

CHAPTER 12
Boundaries

Wait what? What are boundaries? I never knew what boundaries were until I started loving myself again at the age of thirty-seven. Have you ever been in a place where you were afraid to say no or enforce your boundaries because you did not want people to be mad at you? Or you were too nervous to say, "No, this does not work for me," or "No, I cannot do this," or "No, I will not do that"? You even then thought about it and were thinking, *this is my house, or this is my life, I do not have to allow everyone into it.*

If it is stressing you out or causing you to be scared to say no, then it is something you need to rid yourself of. I have learned people who are getting upset with you or mad or annoyed at you for your boundaries are the ones who are benefiting from your lack of boundaries. They are the ones who have been taking advantage of you, intentionally or not. Allowing yourself to say no can be very freeing, but it also can get very lonely because you will soon find out which people were in your life for their own gain.

Boundaries were hard for me to learn and implement. There will also be a time when you start putting boundaries in place and some will try to manipulate you to see if you will bend your boundaries. Sometimes you will bend them until you realize you do not have to keep the peace for the sake of others because it ignites the embers in your soul, and then there is going to be resentment.

Keep in mind your boundaries are not for the other person. They are for you, for you to keep your own peace. It may seem at times that you are putting boundaries in place so that a toxic person will finally learn or listen to your needs, but this will not be the case. Toxic people do not care if there are boundaries; boundaries do not apply to them. Boundaries are incredible and serve a greater purpose than you could ever imagine. Not only did they clear my head, but they created a path for me to focus on me and decide what path I wanted to go down. I had changed. I was different. My mind was different, my outlook was different, my choices were different, and how I behaved was different.

I started to be more intentional with the information I had gathered over the last four years, putting things I had learned to use. I finally set boundaries! That is when I went *no contact*. Something in my mind clicked. I was sick of this shit. I realized my self-worth; I realized I had been doing this thing called life by myself. I realized nobody should be made to feel like they are worthless.

When you are strong in your boundaries, the real healing can begin. You have the possibility to meet the authentic version of yourself. You have the choice to teach people how to treat you. Your time, energy and your vibe are priceless and should only be given out sparingly.

CHAPTER 13
No Contact

This was by far one of the hardest positions I have ever been in, let alone a decision I made, but it served a major part in my healing process. It took me an exceptionally long time to go *no contact*. Your silence can and will speak major volumes. There is no path that is laid out to get to this point. It will be a very bumpy road that you will get lost on and then find your way, if you decide to go this route like I did. Deciding to go no contact will make you feel a tremendous amount of guilt. Making this choice takes bravery and courage and much inner strength, because you will want to go back on your decision.

If you are unfamiliar with what going no contact means, it is a choice that is made to help you heal without continuously breaking your own heart. It creates a space for yourself to grieve the loss of the toxic person and break the cycle of addiction to them. No contact supplies freedom from the trauma: freedom to choose to do as you please, frees you from having consequences, freedom from being blamed, freedom from abuse, and freedom from threats. It allows for time to heal within yourself without any distraction from the toxicity. No contact allows you to make your own decisions, creating space for your thoughts and for your future.

I went from daily communication to deciding one day that I was done. I was not exactly sure what it was that flipped my switch, and I am sure right now you are thinking there is no way you could ever go *no contact*. It is hard. It is painful—I mean physically painful. You will go through withdrawal, maybe not in the physical existence of your person, but from the things that were your normal. All the difficulties, the arguments, the defending yourself, the apologies, the love bombing stages, the little glimpses of hope, the wondering if they will be mad at you or if there will be consequences—all of these are a nightmare.

I did not realize this till I was in therapy discussing it, but I realized the day I went no contact, I made the choice with rational thinking. My decision was not based on any of my emotions. Sometimes, you want to talk to them because you want to say what you forgot to say in a prior call or respond to an email or a text message. Maybe you want to continue the fight, because being without the extreme ups and downs, life doesn't feel normal. You do not feel normal.

I longed for this feeling. There were many times I wanted to turn back. Despite everything that I had gone through with my trauma and loss, I wanted my normal. Same with my brother when he committed suicide: I wanted the communication. I am sure you and people you have relationships with have been through so many things it is only normal that they are your comfort. You know what to expect from them and can determine based on past experiences how they will act or respond in most situations.

My point is that no contact is a mind game. You want someone so bad, but you know they are bad for you, they are toxic for you. But again, that is what is normal, so it supplies comfort. Going no contact provides you space—not only away from your trauma or people involved, but away from the toxic person you also are when in contact with them. Once you get to the point that you can make a rational decision based on things that are factual, in my experience, you are ready to take the leap. Once you control your mind, it becomes much easier to make healthier decisions. It will take you a while to adjust to what your new normal will be, but I promise you, the pain and agony you will go through will be worth it.

You will know when you are completely done with someone or something when you decide that letting go of it and freeing yourself from it is better than feeling like you lost something. You will feel freedom and empowerment.

CHAPTER 14
Forgiveness

Forgiveness was a struggle for me. Why I should have to forgive these people for what was done to me? I learned a few things along the way. Forgiveness does not mean reconciliation. Forgiveness does not mean you have forgotten what has been done to you or things you have endured. Forgiveness *is for you*. Forgiveness is for you to release the toxicity from your body. Forgiving allows *you* to let go of the built-up anger, resentment, and hurt that you hold toward yourself and the person that caused those things for you. Forgiveness does not okay what has been done to you, but it does confirm what has been done to you. Forgiveness allows you the opportunity to change your mindset. Once you forgive, your focus is no longer on that trauma, the loss, or the person. It is no longer about those things. It becomes about you and only you.

Something also to think about when thinking about forgiveness is this: accepting what has happened to you, or what was done to you, or what you have endured. Accept it for what it really is; do not minimize the impact it has had on you. Validate how you felt in those moments and make the conscious decision that forgiving is in your own best interests. It is giving up your right for revenge. If you really think about it, the more time you spend on wanting revenge or wishing ill things on certain people, the more time and energy you have wasted on moments you can never change—time and energy you can never get back.

It took me a while to get to the place of forgiveness and being content with forgiveness can have a noticeably significant impact on how you start to view your situation after the fact of forgiveness. For me, my mindset was different. I was more aware of how things played out, more aware of what was changing about me. People noticing that I was getting my sparkle back in my eyes. For me, forgiveness was a ridiculously hard journey to process, but once I understood that forgiveness was for me, it was much easier for me to understand.

Forgiving someone does not mean you must let them back into your life. You can choose to accept their apology and still have the choice to deny them access to you.

What I have learned is my reality was not actually my reality. It was simply a chapter of my life that was put forth to teach me lessons that I needed to learn and show me things I needed to see. I learned that I was going to have to grieve the loss of this chapter. I lost so many things during this time—many people, places, and relationships. I also lost many personal aspects of myself, and my innocence was lost. I had to forgive myself for the false reality I had allowed myself to portray. I had to forgive myself for not loving myself.

If you had dealt with many kinds of people who were quick to insult, quick to criticize, quick to be abusive and disrespectful. Forgive them. Some of them had no boundaries to what was humanly acceptable. There are a separate set of rules for other people, but those same rules did not apply to them, and God forbid you ever display anything close to their treatment to them. When you do, you are called crazy, you are making things up, and you are insecure. They feed off their own lies. Most people only notice you when you are responding to something that is being done or said to you—which also is reactive abuse. People do not often see you were provoked before your response. Forgive them. This was particularly frustrating because it was not just a one-time offense, and it was hard for me to sit back and watch the nonsense continue.

Here is a question to consider while thinking about forgiveness. Think back to the journey of your relationships, all the difficulties, all the disrespect, the insults, threats, or awful behaviors. Did you forgive the persons, or were you desperate to keep the relationship? Desperate to keep the image? Think about this for a minute. Write down some of your thoughts. If you have experienced loss, are you neglecting yourself forgiveness? If so, why?

_____

_____

_____

_____

CHAPTER 15
The Adventure to You

I had my aha moment in one therapy session, and it felt like someone had run in and dumped a cold cup of water on me while I was in a hot shower. It shocked the shit out of me. We were talking about the week, questions about how the proceedings were going and my brother's birthday. I sat there in silence just looking at my therapist. When she asked me how the proceedings were going, I had told her that I had gotten another response and briefly told her what it was. When she asked me how I felt about it, I said I had not really given it much thought, nor did I respond.

Holy shit! My normal is overthinking, letting my mind spin, thinking about all the things that could go wrong or different outcomes! I told her about my brother's birthday and how we celebrated and such, and in those moments, I realized that I had made a lot of progress! I was beaming and glowing, and I only say this because it was noticeable to my therapist!

She said, "Girl, you did the hard work. I told you if you kept going down your one path, I would not keep working with you!"

Here is what I learned: you cannot heal from trauma when you are still in the trauma. This could be phone calls, letters, emails, or texts, maintaining the same routine as when the trauma happened or being actively involved in things that create chaos for you. Sounds easy and simple, right? You cannot expect change while doing the same thing over and over, expecting different results. Well, it is not easy! People who have experienced trauma or loss, or me personally, often think we are doing the right thing. For me I always feared if I were not complying or doing what I was told, there would be consequences. I lived in fear, and that is the place you are at right now. But I did everything to try to be good enough, none of which had anything to do with the treatment toward me. That was my own issue to deal with.

Back to those subconscious thoughts we have: Everything you choose to do or not to do starts with you. Once you get a better understanding of where you are in your journey and where you are trying to go, things will become clearer. But if you are not going to be vulnerable and open about yourself, the journey to healing will be extremely difficult. Maybe it starts with the decision to start seeing a therapist; maybe it starts with saying aloud something bad has happened to you; maybe it is confiding in a close friend and letting them know you are hurting inside, and the emotions are too heavy to bear. It could be any of those things, but without the choice to make an intent decision geared toward yourself and making yourself better, you will not be able to successfully move forward. I only say this because I have lived it.

If you do not feel like you have a voice, I will be your voice. This statement is a little weird for me. I was insecure and not sure of myself, and I always doubted I knew what I was talking about, even if I had done hundreds of hours of research or had personally experienced it myself. I had a lot of self-doubt. This time it is different. I feel like God put all these obstacles in my life, knowing I would overcome them and be a voice for people who do not have a voice or do not yet know how to use it. Because let us be honest, when you start using your voice, people do not like it. But that is okay. Not everyone is going to like you or agree with what you might say, but they do not get to decide if you can have a voice or not. Speak your truth, use the voice that has been become a new thing to you, take your power back, and regain control over your life.

To be completely honest with you, most people who do not like you or have a problem with what you are using your voice for, most likely do not serve as a positive purpose in your life. Hopefully, my experiences that I have talked about can give you some comfort and strength to know it is okay to have a voice.

When you start to use your voice, here are some things to try and avoid or at least think about. You do not owe anybody or anything a response—least of all a toxic person. Do not respond to things that do not sit right with you. Try your hardest to not point out what someone else is doing wrong. Do not argue with them or try to give your point of view. Doing so is a complete waste of your time and energy. If you do end up falling into this pattern, things will be twisted in favor of the toxic person. Things will be thrown back in your face and used against you. You will once again feel like you are crazy and out of control. You will not know what reality is, and your triggers will come rushing at you with no way to stop them. You will be back at square one, starting over again.

I heard somewhere on a podcast that sometimes people do not take that next step, because once they make that next step, there is no going back. That next step can be scary because it will be new and uncomfortable, and you will not be able to identify with anything anymore because the choice has been made. You made the choice, and you are different now without even knowing it. I did not know I had made the step till I made the step. In addition, taking the step also means that one last thing that connecting you to the person is severed. Of course, you will have setbacks and be sad at times or have memories, but they will not trigger you as they did before. Taking that step puts you into the unknown. It will make you feel uncomfortable. It will make you feel uncertain and scared. But you will not want to turn back.

Taking the next step means you have taken control over your life. It means believing in yourself to make the decision on your own without a co-signer. It means you are finally ready to be the best version of yourself. Taking the next step means you must understand everything with the toxic person is a win-or-lose situation. There is no gray area. They will try to make you emotionally involved in the moment, to distract you from what you are fighting for. They want to trigger your emotions; this is how they continue to control and manipulate you. Understand that a toxic person usually seems bitter when you find your voice or take your power back. They accuse you of betrayal. Toxic people put in a lot of work and effort to make you obey, so going against what they say, angers them.

Have you ever felt so lost that no matter what you did to try to find yourself, it was always a dead end, but you did not realize that the person you were searching for no longer existed? The version of you before the abuse, before the trauma or loss, left you the moment it happened. This was hard for me to come to terms with. I loved most parts of myself before these experiences, but the truth is, the best parts of me are still within me, just in a unique way.

In my mind I think that people will tell you exactly who they are if you just listen. But when I sat down and debated this with myself, I concluded it is completely inaccurate. I believe that you can see what people are trying to show you if you are willing to separate your personal view of them, the view you have of them in your head, from what they are trying to show you. You must be open-minded enough to understand your views in fact could be wrong, or maybe you were completely off, and you had been lying to yourself the whole time. Maybe you were focused on the picture you had painted in your head of how you wanted them to be and were so caught up in that idea you failed to see what was in front of you all along.

This can happen because our pride is too big. Your judgment was off. Maybe you were blinded like I was by the amount of love that I felt for them. Nonetheless, the reality you painted for yourself was wrong.

What change can you make today?

_____

_____

_____

_____

Start small. Do not make the mistake I did and overwhelm yourself and want everything to fall apart at once. Not funny, but I laugh at myself now thinking that was a smart idea. It was not. I can handle anything, but this way of thinking was not the best choice.

It starts with your own actions, your own decisions, your own mindset.

CHAPTER 16
What Your Body Remembers

Let me just say, I do not know what your journey is that you are on, but I am a firm believer in God. I know God is not for everyone, but for me, God spared my life during my assault. During my trauma, I was asked if I was ready to die, and a knife was held above my head, I closed my eyes, and I said, "Okay, God, if this is my time to die, then I am ready!" I was not fearful or scared; to be honest, I froze. After being away from the trauma for a while with no contact, it may sound crazy, but everything that has happened had to happen in the exact order that it did for me to be in this position today. Hopefully, it will make sense once we make it to the end of the book.

Have you ever experienced being in flight, fight, or freeze mode? Maybe you fought back and whooped some ass; maybe you ran and hid; maybe you ran to keep yourself safe. Maybe you were like me and froze and then ran. What was it like for you?

_____

_____

_____

_____

I mentioned freeze mode. I mention this because I never understood what was happening to me during the trauma. I remember trying to play out every scenario in my head and what would happen if I did this or that and what he would do to me if I did those things, so I froze. I did not fight back; I did not try to stop him from punching me in the side of the face or slapping me or hitting me so hard I fell to the ground, only for him to lift me up by my hair and do it again. I knew in my mind that if I fought back, I would not be here today to be authoring this book, and the children would be without their mother. In situations of this nature, I have learned that there is fight, flight, or freeze.

Obviously in my experience, they all suck because if you think about it, you must be in a crappy situation to have to know about these things. I was numb to everything that was going on around me in those moments. It was like I left my own body; sounds crazy, but it is really a thing. Everything sounded muffled, I was there but not reacting. My ears were ringing. There was a lot of commotion but no reaction from me.

It has been best described to me that your brain becomes overwhelmed and disorganized because of the trauma you are experiencing, and your body goes into survival mode, therefore shutting down the higher reasonings of the brain. Then the brain releases hormones to activate the fight, flight, or freeze response to help you survive the trauma. Which makes sense why I did not fight back. I fought myself on this for a long time, and I often wondered what would have happened if I had done things differently in those moments, but I learned that there was nothing I could have done to stop it from happening.

Do you find yourself having regrets about not doing things differently? Those regrets will be a constant battle. What do you think would be your outcome if you had done things differently in those moments?

_____
_____
_____
_____
_____

I was living in a chronic state of survival. My body and my mind were always on high alert. I adapted hyper-vigilance as a coping mechanism. I was always ready to run. I tried hard not to plant deep roots anywhere in fear of having to up and leave again.

I had dealt with many forms of abuse such as manipulation, being hit, being slapped, sexual abuse, control, financial control, torment, and verbal threats. I also learned that people who display these kinds of things have no self-esteem, nor do they have control. In the end, I ended up with Stockholm syndrome. Stockholm syndrome is defined by WebMD as an emotional response that happens to some abuse victims when they experience positive feelings toward their toxic person. I became emotionally dysregulated. I stopped loving me, and that was a problem. When I started to lose myself, I started to lose the way in which I love. I love hard, and I am all in, so when we did not work, I took on the blame. I told myself that it was because of my shortcomings.

My body responded to all the things I have endured and each one has a different reaction. Now that I am aware what the emotion is and what symptom the emotion is triggering, I has been so much easier to manage. Not only manage being able to better train my brain that I am not in danger.

Add self-care into your normal routine. Self-care is also noticing how your body is feeling. Suppressing emotions can have a detrimental effect on your body. I was getting sick every time I ate or drank something. I could never figure out why until after I was away from the trauma. I learned that my body's response was due to the trauma and triggers I was experiencing.

CHAPTER 17
Triggers

I have learned that my body remembers emotions and thoughts of the scariest time of my life. Triggers are relevant when trying to heal from trauma. The anniversary date of my survivor date is a major trigger. A year had passed, but I could not make sense of why my body was feeling so nervous or why I was sad and mad all at the same time. This only really made sense to me after I read the book *The Body Keeps the Score* written by Bessel van der Kolk, MD. It is an amazing book that I highly recommend you read. There is a great deal of beneficial information in this book.

I mentioned earlier that for a significant period, I was getting sick every time I ate or drank something, and I could never figure out why, until after I was away from the trauma. What I have learned is that I was so anxious and stressed out that my body was physically reacting to the trauma. I went to several doctors and could not figure it out. I eventually was diagnosed with PTSD and anxiety, and since I have been *no contact*, I have not been as sick. My anxiety was through the roof, and my stress level was always on high alert, and it did not help that I never knew what was going on.

I have dealt with a lot of triggers because of the trauma, but they can be manageable after you recognize what they are and all the ways they affect you mentally, emotionally, and physically. I dealt with many triggers after the extreme trauma: the sight of an ambulance driving past the place I lived in where the act happened, the sight of bright yellow construction coats, squad cars, the sight of certain knives; also dates surrounding the trauma and the death of my brother, things that remind me of how he died, the death of my best friend, the place on the road where she was killed, or other events that had a major impact on me.

What are some of the emotions that you are feeling in this moment as you read the text? What kind of things is your body experiencing right now?

_____

_____

_____

_____

CHAPTER 18
Things to Remember

I learned that you must control your mind to be stronger than your emotions. If you do not, you will lose the battle every time. You must, and I mean *must* come to a place where you stop waiting to be this perfect version of yourself that you have pictured in your head; that person no longer exists. You must acknowledge your flaws and your strengths and enjoy them for what they are in the moment. Your flaws and strengths will vary moment by moment; embrace them and own them. They are a part of you, no matter what you try to do to erase them.

If you are anything like me and have struggled to figure out how to heal, trying to figure out what that means or what that looks like daily—then let me encourage you not to overthink it. Healing does not have a road map. Healing is messy and confusing. But healing *does not* mean you are not allowed to take care of yourself. You are allowed not to be doing anything. You are allowed to stay home with the curtains closed and not answer any emails, phone calls, or texts.

You are allowed to do things that make you feel better in the moment. Be aware, though, that this can also turn into a distraction, as we already discussed. I want to allow you to visualize diverse ways of how to think about things, not tell you what to think. How to think gives you freedom to think for yourself, not how you are told what to think.

Pay attention to the advice people are offering. Does it give you the choice to choose your own path or only their own? Unconditional love is loving someone for who they are. These people are the ones you most likely trust. Avoid people who mess with your head and mess with your emotions, people who intentionally do things that they know upset you. Avoid people who expect you to make them a priority but treat you like a possibility. Understand that you cannot grow until your mindset changes. You cannot grow in the place that crushed you. Sometimes growing means new friends, a new location, or a new view of yourself.

You must get to a place where your peace of mind becomes a priority. Protecting your peace is a form of self-care. Understand that you cannot make healthy decisions with an unhealthy mind.

You must get to a place where you are at peace with accepting the fact that you may never get an apology. Honestly, even if you got an apology, it would not change the fact that you are healing on your own. An apology does not get to have control of your healing. You must give yourself some grace, no matter how much guilt you carry. You cannot change the past, and no amount of worry can change the present. Prepare yourself to expect that things will become extremely uncomfortable as you begin to heal. Try your hardest not to fall back into what is comfortable. When you find yourself apologizing, stop yourself, and embrace the discomfort.

Part of the healing process is taking the time to understand how toxic you are as a person. It is hard for people to face their real selves and acknowledge what parts of them they need to fix or heal. Remember you are resilient. Remember you are responsible for your own healing path; you are not responsible for anything but yourself. In the same way, nobody else is responsible for your happiness or peace. You get to choose who you allow in your life; you get to choose what characteristics you allow in your life; you get to decide if something is healthy for you. And the bonus! You do not owe anyone an explanation. You get to be in control of your life.

One of the greatest recognitions is some people never change, and that is their own journey, and there is no place in their journey for you to try and fix them; nor is it your responsibility. You cannot save anyone from themselves. They must choose themselves. I need you to choose yourself. I need you to say, "I choose me. I choose my life, I choose my happiness, and I choose my sanity. I choose to love myself, starting today." You can be healing and hurting at the same time. They do not need to be mutually exclusive. No response *is* a response, and not everything is entitled to a response.

IMAGINE

- Imagine finally finding the strength and courage to leave and cut ties with a toxic person.
- Imagine being able to navigate through the emotions and the trauma you have experienced.
- Imagine understanding how you ended up in this situation in the first place.
- Imagine being able to recognize all the bullshit and untrue allegations about yourself that have been engrained into your head from your toxic person.
- Imagine finding the perfect therapist.
- Imagine working through your trauma and making good out of it.
- Imagine using your story to help another person with theirs.
- Imagine loving yourself again.
- Imagine educating yourself enough to be able to put your pieces back together.
- Imagine being happy and at peace again.
- Imagine falling in love with someone who loves all your broken pieces.
- Imagine being with someone who encourages you to be a better person.

Imagine being able to do all these things, what would that mean for you?

_____
_____
_____
_____
_____
_____
_____

Things in my control

- My emotions
- My responses
- My behaviors
- My thought processes
- Where I invest my time
- Who I give my energy to
- My goals
- My habits
- The way I talk to myself
- My boundaries
- My ability to be present
- How well I listen and comprehend

Things out of my control

- Others negativity
- Actions of others
- What someone thinks about me
- Opinions of others
- How someone else responds
- Change
- Other people's happiness

- Other people's beliefs
- The past
- The future

Not being able to control all aspects of life creates much uncertainty, but also allows for much beauty. The beauty of not being able to control, makes for letting go to be easier. Letting go of control makes it easier to make decisions. There is no way to predict anything that may or not may happen. Letting go of control allows for different opportunities to become present and more space in your mind to think more freely.

The scars that you are carrying are your proof that you have made it this far. Wear those scars like war paint. You are stronger than the things that have been sent to break you. Destroy and break every single fucking chain that supplies access to you that is causing you harm. The obstacle has come; it has served its purpose. Now it is up to you to learn the lesson.

Every single choice has a destination. Sometimes we do not know the impact of the choice, but it will lead you on a path that is essentially life or death. Is the choice helping you grow, or is it killing a part of who you are meant to be? You get to choose; you have a choice. Healing yourself from the downside up will feel like you are in a hole so deep that there is no conceivable way to get out. It is as if you are at the bottom of a canyon, and you see all the potential obstacles in front of you, and you want to quit repeatedly, but you do not, because there will be a slight glimpse of hope. That hope will guide you to keep putting one foot in front of the other. It is during these times that you will be rebuilding the foundation to yourself. Build the foundation to yourself so strong that there is nothing that can stop you from achieving your end goal—the end goal of healing and being successful on your journey.

Give yourself some credit for how far you have come. If nobody has told you lately, I am proud of you. Let me tell you why!

You are here, reading this book with the hope you will learn something or notice a different way of thinking. Reading to gather information is a huge step in the right direction, even if it seems minor. Your mind could be trying to grasp for any glimpse of hope. I am hoping that reading my story will provide you with the hope you are looking for.

Repeat after me! "I love myself despite what I have endured. My chaos is not my reality. Thank you for loving me. Thank you for trying your best to protect me."

Hold on, beautiful soul, I will be here to help you look beyond your situation and notice promises in disguise. I will be here to see hope when you feel hopeless. I will be here to point out the potential in your pain. I will be here to supply guidance when you feel lost.

CHAPTER 19
My Lessons

I am a single parent to four children who are my world. I learned that I had the strength it took inside of me to be hurting and healing while caring for the children. I took on the challenge of creating a life I did not have to run from in the hopes that the children would never have to deal with something so horrific again in their lives. I have gotten to experience the transformations of the children as they work through their trauma and have watched them implement things that they have been learning. I had the opportunity to cheer on one of the children for writing their own book on their version of their trauma. I learned that consistency is key for the children and me to keep moving forward on our journey to healing.

I do not have it figured all out. I take on things as they come. I have learned to accept things for what they are and deal with things accordingly with the information I have in that moment.

I learned to let people do what they are going to do and not take it personally.

I have a love for how the mind works. I have a bachelor's degree in Psychology, some say this is dangerous, but I believe in the contrary. I love to keep learning and studying or researching things I do not understand.

I am so proud of myself for how I have handled all the chaos and mess that I have endured. Proud of how much I have evolved and grown into this confident and secure woman as opposed to the insecure little girl I used to be.

I learned that I did not lose myself during all my mess. Who I needed was inside of me all along, I just had to unlearn unhealthy coping mechanisms and response tactics that were no longer beneficial for me. I had to unlearn survival tactics that no longer served a purpose.

I learned how to forgive myself for not knowing better in those moments. I learned to forgive myself for being who I needed to be to survive. I learned to forgive myself for not knowing how to implement boundaries and for not using my own voice.

I learned that I needed a healthy support system. I learned that I needed to ask for help and reach out and grab a hand that was reached out to me. I learned that asking for help is not a weakness. It is courageous and bold.

I learned that just a glimpse of hope with the fire in my soul to fight the battle is all I needed to overcome my shame and humiliation.

I learned that despite all the ugly that I have experienced that I still love like I have never been hurt. I decided to give up my right for revenge and decided to thrive. The best revenge for me was to not worry about revenge and work through my story and be genuinely happy. I learned to not focus on the things that are going on around me.

I learned that I have a choice in every single situation or circumstance. I learned that I can be healing and hurting at the same time. I learned that I have the right to live in a calm environment that is free of chaos and destruction.

I learned that if someone cannot be transparent with themselves about their own flaws that they lack self-awareness. I learned self-awareness for myself. I stood in the mirror, faced the ugly truths about myself, and learned my own toxic patterns.

I learned that my trauma will always be apart of me. My triggers still show up at random times, but instead of being in froze mode, I acknowledge the trigger and I thank my body and my mind for cautioning me for danger. I learned to validate my emotions regardless of what they are.

I learned that I have strength, generosity, humility, compassion, respect, courage, determination, boldness, honesty, and truth at my core.

I am not fighting for a spot in anyone's life anymore. My biggest flex, besides my ass, is that I love to see other people succeeding. I love making small gestures to show people that I see them, more so that they are seen. I love appreciating another woman's beauty. Even more, I love witnessing someone recover from something that was meant to break them. Having the ability to create something beautiful out of something so ugly is priceless. There is such a pure, genuine beauty in seeing the transformation. I am rooting for you. I am cheering you on to be successful in your journey.

ACKNOWLEDGMENTS

I must say thank you and give credit and praise where it is due. First, I thank God for sparing my life.

I am extremely thankful for my parents who made the choice to raise me with God in my life. Not to mention the stability that they provided through this whole shit show.

I want to say thank you to my family, especially my siblings. I cannot express how blessed I am to have the siblings that I have and the power and strength that transpires when we are together.

My children, I am your biggest fan. You are my ride-or-die humans. You require characteristics from me that you can also offer to me.

My best friends, friends, lost friends, and acquaintances: I have learned something from each one of you. It may not have been the best lesson, but a lesson that was needed. I am grateful for all the love and support that I have gotten on my journey.

I would like to extend my deepest gratitude to my loss and trauma. Without you and the obstacles, I would not have known where I needed to heal. I have managed to take everything that you have thrown my way and overcome it. I would like to express gratitude to those who believed in me when I could not believe in myself.

And I would like to pay special regard to my baby brother Porter. You taught me to fight for my life by showing me that the pain we feel when we lose someone we love, is worth fighting through. You provided me with pure, genuine love, and I will be forever grateful.

And lastly, *you*, reader: Thank you for taking the time to read my shit show. I hope it gives you a glimpse of hope.

"God is within her; she will not fail." —Psalm 46:5

In loving memory of my brother

February 20, 1994–May 24, 2020

My loving brother, you have taught me to love myself more, to enjoy the awkward things and embrace who I am, and that starts with loving myself. You have shown me the best and the worst sides of yourself, and I love them all equally. I would not be who I am or love how I love without having you as a part of my journey.

My funniest memory of you is when you were about fourteen years old. I was on my way to class, driving along, and I saw Grandma's car sitting on the side of a gravel road. It was you! —you little shit, just out for a joy ride. I had you get in with me, and I drove you back home. I was honestly a little jealous of you that you had the balls to drive around on a gravel road at fourteen. You were not even fearful of getting in trouble.

You had so many God-given talents! I loved watching you play football and play sports. You were great at everything you did.

I admire your fierceness, your soft heart, and most of all your smirk. I love you with all my heart, and I miss the shit out of you! Until we meet again, Porter Willy Ham. I will fight to make you proud.

NEVER TRULY BROKEN

Dear Future Self,

I know those past years have been extremely hard. You thought the chapter would never end. You made it! I am so proud of you for overcoming all the obstacles that were thrown your way with the intentions to break you. You are one badass bitch.

I hope you are smiling as you read this and think back about how far you have come and all the things through which you have worked. I hope you when you look back at this point in your life that you understand that everything you went through was worth it.

Stand firm in your truth and remind yourself you are an overcomer. You did it. You won. You won yourself back, and you fought like hell to save yourself. You are incredible and beautiful. When people speak negatively of you, that has everything to do with them.

Remember that change can be good, struggles teach you a lesson, and you make yourself stronger and wiser.

Your life down the road will be much better than you could have ever imagined. There will be a prince charming and more love and joy that you have experienced. Take a breath and enjoy this journey now. Good things will continue to come.

Stay strong; stay loyal to what is true for you. You matter, your voice matters, your life matters. Fuck what anyone else says. Throw plot twists around like confetti. You know your end goal and work towards it every single day.

Xoxo —Present Self

"I am not perfect, nor do I seek perfection, only to have a better understanding of myself."